the khrushchev era

1953 -1965

by Stuart A. Kallen

Consultant: Margaret Robinson Preska, Ph.D. Russian History
President, Mankato State University [1979-1992]

Published by Abdo & Daughters, 6535 Cecilia Circle, Edina, Minnesota 55439.

Copyright © 1992 by Abdo Consulting Group, Inc., Pentagon Tower, P.O. Box 36036, Minneapolis, Minnesota 55435. International copyrights reserved in all counties. No part of this book may be reproduced in any form without written permission from the publisher. Printed in the United States.

Photo credits: Archive Photos-6, 8, 9, 12, 19, 23, 28, 30, 31, 36, 42, 46, 48
                   FPG International-cover, 40
                   Globe Photos-15, 33

Edited by: Rosemary Wallner

Library of Congress Cataloging-in-Publication Data

Kallen, Stuart A., 1955-
     The Khrushchev era / written by Stuart A. Kallen ; [edited by Rosemary Wallner].
          p. cm. — (The Rise & fall of the Soviet Union)
     Includes index.
     Summary: Examines events in the Soviet Union during the era of Khrushchev, with an emphasis on his political reforms.
     ISBN 1-56239-103-8 (lib. bdg.)
     1. Soviet Union—Politics and government—1953-1985—Juvenile literature. 2. Khrushchev, Nikita Sergeevich, 1894-1971—Juvenile literature. [1. Soviet Union—Politics and government—1953-1985. 2. Khrushchev, Nikita Sergeevich, 1894-1971.] I. Wallner, Rosemary, 1964- . II. Title. III. Series: Kallen, Stuart A., 1955- Rise & fall of the Soviet Union.
DK274.K294 1992
947.085'2—dc20   92-13476
                                                                          CIP
                                                                          AC

18401

table of contents

showdown over cuba

t was a crisp fall morning in 1962. An emergency siren's shrieking whoop shattered the stillness. The men in the Strategic Air Command (SAC) dropped whatever they were doing and ran down into their bunkers. It was from there, fifty feet below the Nebraska prairie that World War III would be fought. These soldiers had been tested and trained over and over for this moment. It was a red alert and dozens of fingers hovered over the buttons that could unleash America's thermonuclear weapons. For the next two weeks the soldiers at SAC remained poised over their nuclear code-books. Meanwhile diplomats and politicians shuttled about the globe dragging the world back from the brink of nuclear disaster.

On October 16, 1962, United States President John F. Kennedy had been alerted that the Soviet Union was building ten missile bases on the island of Cuba, ninety miles off the coast of Florida. United States' spy planes had photographed forty medium-ranged nuclear missiles.

Each one of those missiles was fifty times stronger than the atomic bombs that had been dropped on Japan in World War II. Those missiles could reach Washington, D.C., in thirty minutes. In addition, there were twelve even larger intermediate-range missiles that could strike Canada; one hundred forty surface-to-air missiles; forty Soviet jet bombers; and twenty thousand Soviet soldiers and advisors. This news was extremely startling, and Kennedy put the United States military on full alert.

Kennedy went on television to give the grave facts to a fearful American public. Kennedy told Americans that the United States Navy would blockade Cuba and inspect every Soviet ship that was planning to dock there. Ships containing weapons or military supplies would be turned back. Kennedy also told the Soviet Union that any missiles launched from Cuba would be regarded as a Soviet attack on the United States. Kennedy warned that this would warrant "a full scale response against the Soviet Union."

In the Soviet capital of Moscow, Nikita Khrushchev, the leader of the Soviet Union, responded angrily. Khrushchev denounced Kennedy's speech and said the United States was "provoking" the Soviet Union.

U.S. President John F. Kennedy addressing the
nation on television during the Cuban Missile Crisis, 1962.

Kennedy put SAC on full alert, sent troops to Florida, and sent Polaris submarines out on top-secret courses. Suddenly, Americans were glued to their radios and televisions, nervously waiting out the war of nerves. Some Americans began digging fallout shelters that they mistakenly thought would protect them from nuclear bombs. There were runs at hardware and grocery stores as frightened people stocked up on food, water, candles, bullets, and other items deemed necessary in the coming holocaust.

Within days, sixty American battleships stood in a line five hundred miles off the coast of Cuba. They had orders to sink any ship that would not submit to inspection. Meanwhile, twenty Soviet vessels steamed toward Cuba, about to rendezvous with destiny. The whole world watched uneasily.

When the ships met the blockade, they were turned back. The crisis was over. Secretary of State Dean Rusk said, "We went eyeball to eyeball, and the other fellow blinked." Khrushchev wired Kennedy and offered to dismantle the bases if the United States removed their missiles from Turkey. Kennedy refused. (Six months later however, the missiles were removed from Turkey.)

An American family in their well stocked fallout shelter. Families were told to have enough food and water to last two weeks.

A Soviet freighter is stopped by a U.S. Navy destroyer off the Cuban coast in 1962.

Khrushchev then offered to remove the missile bases if Kennedy ended the blockade and pledged not to invade Cuba. Kennedy welcomed the agreement. Thus ended the most nerve-wracking confrontation ever between the two nuclear superpowers.

Kennedy's popularity soared as Americans rallied around their strong-willed leader. In Moscow though, Nikita Khrushchev had been humiliated. It would not be long until he was out of a job.

superpower opposites

At the time of the Cuban Missile Crisis, the United States and the Soviet Union were the two most powerful nations on Earth. But the leaders of these two superpowers could not have been more different. President Kennedy was a young, handsome man who had been born into great wealth and power. A natural leader, Kennedy's rise to the top had been quick and easy. He never lost an election, and by 1960, he was America's youngest president.

Nikita Khrushchev, on the other hand, was born in 1894 to poor peasants in a small town in the Soviet Union. Because his family was so poor, he worked in the mines when he was only fourteen years old. He became a machinist and worked twelve-hour days when he was still in his teens. Khrushchev had come up through the ranks in the Communist Party for thirty years. This was at a time when a person could be shot just for saying the wrong thing.

Presi

Khrushchev was sixty-six years old by the time of the Missile Crisis. He was a short, stocky, bald man and those who knew him either deeply respected him or despised him. Photographs showing Kennedy and Khrushchev meeting for the first time demonstrate how opposite these two men were.

The United States and the Soviet Union were also two very different countries. World War II had left the United States the richest country on Earth. Many well-fed Americans enjoyed an unheard of prosperity, awash in new cars, homes, and consumer goods. The Soviet Union had been practically destroyed by the war. Over twenty million people had died, and in some parts of the country, the effects of that war were still obvious fifteen years after its end.

The two things that kept the United States and the Soviet Union equal were their large armies and huge stockpile of nuclear weapons, which they pointed at each other. In a battle of words and nerves, this confrontation was called the Cold War. The threat of nuclear annihilation cast a shadow over the whole planet.

general nikita

ikita Khrushchev had come to power in 1953 after the death of Joseph Stalin. For almost thirty years, Stalin had ruled the Soviet Union with an iron fist. In the 1930's he created a man-made famine that starved over twenty million Soviet citizens. After that, Stalin purged the Communist Party of enemies real and imagined. His secret police set up slave labor and prison camps in the frozen wastelands of Siberia. Millions of people were arrested, tortured, and shot at the command of Stalin's secret police force.

When World War II started, the Soviet losses were far greater because Stalin had killed seventy percent of the officers in the Soviet Red Army. Khrushchev fought many long and bloody battles as a commander in World War II. He was in charge of the troops that defeated the German army in Stalingrad.

Nikita Khrushchev ruled the Ukraine with absolute power.

This was a defeat in the war that Germany would never recover from. Khrushchev was made a Lieutenant General and given several military medals.

When the war was over, Khrushchev continued to wear his general's uniform even after he became president of the Soviet state of Ukrainia. The war was over, but the Ukraine was destroyed. People were forced to sow their fields with little more than a hoe and shovel. Because most of the horses, oxen, and donkeys had been killed in the fighting, women were often seen pulling plows. Mines and power stations were deserted, and the railways and roads were destroyed.

Khrushchev ruled the Ukraine with absolute power. Stalin, while striking terror into the hearts of even the strongest men, seemed to be quite pleased with Khrushchev. Unfortunately for the Soviet people, a drought descended on the Ukraine in 1947, and another killer famine gripped the region. Khrushchev appealed to Moscow for help in setting up soup kitchens to ward off starvation. Stalin replied with an abusive telegram relieving Khrushchev of his duties as president of the Ukraine.

Although demoted, Stalin still favored Khrushchev. During the celebration of Stalin's seventieth birthday at the Bolshoi Theater, Khrushchev was allowed to sit next to Stalin. The only other person allowed that honor that night was Mao Tse-tung, the Communist leader of China.

the power shifts

For almost thirty years, Joseph Stalin was the only leader of the Soviet Union. When he died in 1953, he left no one to take his place. In the final years of his life, he had trusted no one, not even his closest advisors. Stalin gave little thought as to who would succeed him, and in fact, when he died, he was planning yet another bloody purge of the Communist Party.

In the immediate wake of Stalin's death, several men stepped in to fill his shoes.

One of them was the head of the secret police. But he was arrested on the spot before he could organize his police forces for a takeover. Later, he was executed. For a while, a group of men ruled, traveling everywhere together to show unity. To show equality, they all traveled together in one official car, piling in and out of the overloaded sedan. In the end, it was Nikita Khrushchev who rose to the top of the Soviet power structure.

setting free the prisoners

hen Stalin died, tens of millions of political prisoners were still suffering in prison camps. These people had been jailed on phony charges. Putting them back into society would be a complicated problem. Not only must the innocent be given their freedom, but they must be given back their jobs, their former lives, and their dignity. The men in charge of arresting those people were still in positions of power all over the country. Under Stalin, if a person was convicted of a crime, his or her entire family was evicted from their home. The family was also banished from schools, the military, and most jobs.

In 1953, thirteen million people lived in Soviet concentration camps. The government set about reviewing every single case. New trials were held, witnesses summoned, evidence presented, and so on. This process was agonizingly slow and ridiculous for people who had been imprisoned for crimes such as complaining about their starvation.

Only four thousand prisoners were released that year. The next year, Khrushchev released about 12,000 people from the camps. These people had been powerful in the Communist Party before Stalin's mass arrests. When Khrushchev released them, his popularity soared and his position secured.

the secret speech

n February 1956, the Twentieth Party Congress opened in the Kremlin. This was a meeting of government officials from all over the Soviet Union. Just before midnight on February 25, Khrushchev delivered a four-hour secret speech entitled "On the Cult of Personality" to 1,500 Communist Party delegates. In the speech, Khrushchev told of Stalin's imprisonment of thousands of innocent people, the torture and execution of devoted and innocent Party leaders, and the grave and costly mistakes made during the war. The list of cruelty and mass repression stunned the audience.

The speech did not remain secret for long. Soon, the headlines of the world flashed the crimes of the world's most brutal dictator, Stalin. At meetings all over the Soviet Union, faithful Communists gathered in shock and pain to hear the speech read by local officials. Soon a program of "de-Stalinization" was started to erase the lies of Stalin.

Khrushchev delivered a four-hour speech entitled "On the Cult of Personality". He told of all of Stalin's torture and executions.

Soviet history was quickly rewritten to remove Stalin's name from many important events.

News of Stalin's crimes fueled public demand for large-scale prison releases. In 1956-1957, over eight million people were released from slave labor camps. Of the tens of millions arrested in the Terror of 1937-38, only five percent were still alive. Six million dead people also had their convictions overturned. This meant that their surviving relatives could now get homes, schools, and jobs. Overturning millions of prison convictions had a profound effect on Soviet society. Victims of prison camps were often given better jobs then other people. The widows of military men who had been murdered received monetary bonuses and pensions. German soldiers who had been taken prisoner more than a decade earlier were finally released.

Khrushchev's leading role in the release of political prisoners earned him great popularity. Nevertheless, two attempts were made on his life during this time. Neither attempt was reported by the Soviet press. In the second attempt, a navy ship Khrushchev was on blew up moments after he had left it. The people trying to kill Khrushchev were men who had helped Stalin in his bloody reign of terror.

When Khrushchev released the prisoners, many of them wanted revenge on the men who put them in the camps. Some of Stalin's henchmen lost their jobs, others were murdered or "disappeared." The fact that Khrushchev had helped Stalin carry out his terror seemed to have been forgotten. Demands for fair trials and the release of secret police documents went unheeded by Khrushchev.

khrushchev's crackdowns

The winds of truth blowing out of the Kremlin fueled many fires. Riots swept across the Soviet state of Georgia as millions tried to grasp the truth of Stalin's rampage. There were also minor revolts in Poland. The country of Hungary had been under Stalin's boot heel since 1946. On October 23, 1956, thousands of young Hungarians marched into Parliament Square in Budapest. That night they pulled down a huge statue of Stalin and broke it into tiny pieces. Fittingly, the only thing left of the statue were Stalin's boots. Feelings of euphoria swept across Hungary as a newly formed government declared its independence from the Soviet Union. The party ended on November 1, when fifteen Red Army divisions entered Hungary, backed up by 5,000 tanks. On November 4, in the middle of the night, the tanks entered Budapest. The Red Army quashed the revolt and killed 25,000 Hungarians in the process. Khrushchev and the Red Army were soundly condemned throughout the world.

The pace of de-Stalinization was not fast enough for authors who hoped for freedom of expression in the Soviet Union. Author Boris Pasternak finished the book *Doctor Zhivago* in 1955. He could not get it published in his own country. The novel was smuggled into Italy and published. Within two years the book was a world-wide best-seller and had been translated into twenty languages. In 1958, Pasternak was given the Nobel Prize in Literature. Inside the Soviet Union, *Doctor Zhivago* was one of the first books photographed page by page and read in secret.

Two days after Pasternak received the Nobel Prize, he was viciously attacked in the Soviet press. The next day, Pasternak was thrown out of the writer's union, which meant he could no longer work as an author. His girl-friend also lost her job. Pasternak cracked, and returned the Nobel Prize. He died of cancer in 1960, a broken man.

Boris Pasternak, the author of Doctor Zhivago.

the race into space

I n August 1957, the Soviet Union announced that they had successfully fired their first inter-continental ballistic missile (ICBM). This meant that the Soviet Union could now launch hydrogen bombs across the oceans. This put the United States on the possible receiving end of a Soviet nuclear missile. A few weeks later, on October 5, the Soviets became the first country to launch a rocket into space. The rocket, called *Sputnik*, made the first successful orbit of Earth, two hundred miles above the planet. One month later *Sputnik 2* carried the first living creature into space. The cargo of the spaceship was a mongrel dog named Laika. Sadly, the rocket had no re-entry capsule, and space-dog Laika drifted off into the void.

The man who had designed *Sputnik* was Sergei Korolev, but he took none of the international glory. In a classic case of Soviet science, his name was kept secret until he died in 1966. Soviet rocket research had begun as early as 1930.

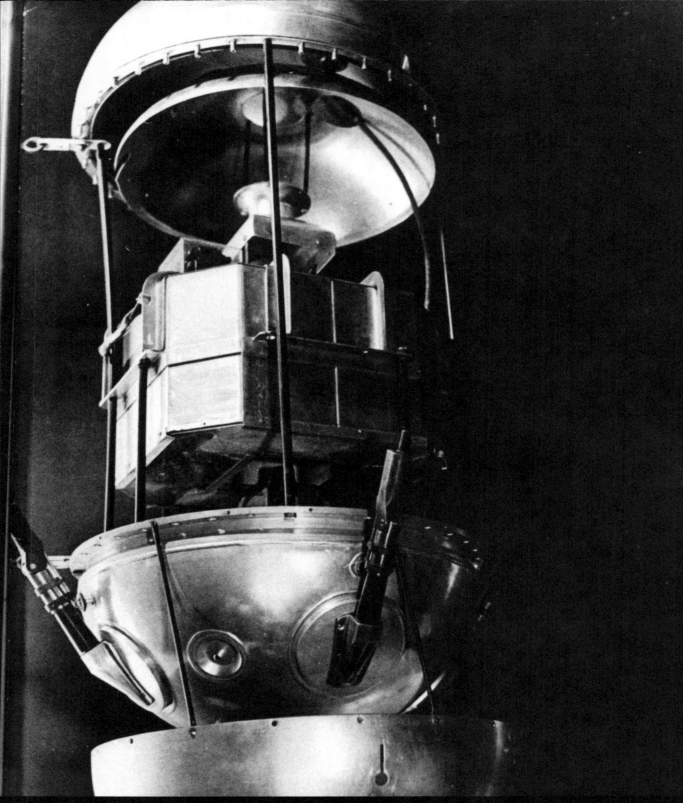

Sputnik; the first rocket to successfully orbit the Earth in 1957.

The Russian dog "Laika" was sent into space in *Sputnik 2*.

But Stalin had most of the scientists shot at the height of his murderous purges. Korolev was one of the millions swept into the slave labor camps in 1937. He was put to work with other aircraft and rocket designers at a special prison. During the war, Stalin worked these imprisoned scientists until they dropped.

Korolev was in prison until 1953. Then he was put to work building missiles under the watchful eye of future Soviet leader Leonid Brezhnev. At first Khrushchev could not understand the purpose of these missiles. "When Korolev showed us one of his rockets," Khrushchev wrote, "it looked like nothing but a huge cigar-shaped tube. We didn't think it would fly. We were like peasants in the marketplace. We walked around the rocket, touching it, tapping it to see if it was sturdy enough — we did everything but lick it to see how it tasted."

Soon enough, Khrushchev became a believer in Korolev's mysterious rockets. The new military hardware meant that the Soviet Union would need fewer soldiers. Its success also did wonders for Khrushchev's political standing. Using it, Khrushchev raised his own prestige, saved money, tamed the Red Army, and threatened the United States.

Sergei Korolev, chief architect of Soviet space technology

The program was pushed ahead at break-neck speed. By the end of 1957, the United States had launched its own ICBM. But the fear of Soviet missiles raining down on the United States increased paranoia and fueled a multi-trillion dollar arms race that profoundly affected the world.

nikita can't go to disneyland

On September 13, 1959, the un-manned Soviet rocket *Lunik II* landed on the moon. The same day, Moscow newspapers announced, "Khrushchev to visit the USA." The visit was truly historic. No leader of the Soviet Communist government had ever visited the United States. But tensions between the two superpowers had been thawing. Earlier in the year, a Soviet exhibition was held in New York City and an American exhibition was held in Moscow. The exhibitions showed how people lived in each country. Vice-President Richard Nixon attended the opening of the American exhibition in Moscow with Khrushchev. It featured a standard American one-story house complete with a modern kitchen, living room, and bathroom. Khrushchev was not impressed.

During the two weeks Khrushchev was in the United States, the press followed him everywhere. The more people scrutinized the gnome-like Soviet leader, the more his popularity grew. All was not smiles though.

Khrushchev and Eisenhower in the U.S.
The two men promised to end the Cold War.

In many cities on his tour, people held signs that read "Khrushchev, the butcher of Hungary," and "Khrushchev — six million starved in the Ukraine in famine he planned with Stalin."

Khrushchev had lunch at the White House with President Dwight D. Eisenhower where the two men promised to end the Cold War. Later in the week, Khrushchev gave a speech at the United Nations. The highlight of his trip was a visit to Hollywood. There, Bob Hope, Henry Fonda, Elizabeth Taylor, Marilyn Monroe, and other Hollywood bigwigs wined and dined him. Monroe shook Khrushchev's hand and later said she was grateful that she didn't have to kiss him because of his warts. At the party Khrushchev complained that he was not allowed to visit Disneyland. "What have you got there?" he whined, "Rocket launching pads? Is there an epidemic there? Have gangsters taken over the place?...What must I do now — commit suicide?"

At the end of the U.S. whirlwind tour, Khrushchev tramped through corn fields in Iowa and visited a meat-packing plant. Arrangements were made to exchange American farming techniques with the ever-hungry Soviet Union.

Khrushchev's trip to the United States also eased tensions in Europe, and he later visited France to a booming reception. Plans were made for Khrushchev to meet with the leaders of the United States, France, and Great Britain to discuss disarmament. Late in 1959, it looked like the Cold War was ending. Any thought of celebration was cut short on May 1, 1960.

the u-2 incident

n the mid-1950's the U-2 airplane was America's biggest secret. Since July 1956, the Central Intelligence Agency (CIA) had been sending the specially designed black, unmarked planes into Soviet airspace. These single-seat aircraft flew 70,000 feet above Soviet air and missile bases, submarine docks, factories, railroads and atomic testing grounds. From fifteen miles up in the air, huge cameras swung from side to side photographing all of the Soviet's secrets. The CIA director bragged that the U-2 could photograph a Soviet general's license plate from twelve miles up in the air. He claimed that he had looked at every blade of grass in the Soviet Union.

Cramped and sweating, staggering out of their pressurized flight suits, the CIA pilots brought back a treasure trove of film, tapes, and other materials for the CIA. The missions were so secret that the pilots could not tell anyone that they had broken the world's altitude records.

39

When Eisenhower authorized U-2 flights over the Soviet Union, he was assured by his advisors that the planes would never crash on Soviet soil. If a plane did go down, he was told, the pilot must throw two switches. Then he would have seventy seconds to eject before an explosive blew up the cameras and other spy equipment. If a crash did occur, NASA would issue a cover story announcing that a "weather plane" had crashed. Privately, no one thought the pilot would live through the ordeal any way.

Francis Gary Powers was singled out of his group of Air Force pilots by the CIA in 1955. In 1956, Powers became the first person to fly a U-2 from Turkey into the Soviet Union and back. The pilots knew that the Soviets were tracking them on radar. Occasionally a Soviet missile came uncomfortably close. On May 1, 1960, the Soviet Union held its annual May Day celebration. To the Soviets, May Day is the most respected national holiday after the October Revolution holiday. On that day, the leaders of the Soviet Union stand atop the walls of the Kremlin and watch the tanks, missiles, and soldiers of the Red Army roll by. Red Square is decorated with banners and bunting celebrating the Soviet glory of the Communist revolution.

Francis Powers of the U.S. Air Force, pilot of the U-2 plane

While Khrushchev reviewed his military hardware that day, Francis Gary Powers flew deep into Soviet airspace. Some 1,300 miles into the country, his automatic pilot mechanism malfunctioned. Powers decided to fly the aircraft manually. Once over a Soviet air force base, Powers switched on his spy cameras. Suddenly he felt a tremendous jolt. The plane went into a spin. Powers was thrown sideways and could not hit the destruct buttons. As the plane plummeted to earth, Powers baled out. In the middle of the May Day parade, Khrushchev learned that a U-2 had been shot down.

At the time of the U-2 crash, most Americans knew nothing about the CIA. Over the next few days, a series of American statements and contradictions gave the people an idea of what their government was up to. On May 2, an official announced that an American "weather plane" was lost over Turkey. The next day it was announced that a "weather plane" may have been forced down in the Soviet Union. On May 5, eleven days before a planned superpower summit, Khrushchev angrily revealed that an American spy plane had been captured. Washington countered that all U-2 "weather flights" would be suspended for two weeks.

A State Department spokesman said that there was "no deliberate attempt to violate Soviet airspace." A day later Khrushchev countered that the flight had been a spy mission and to prove it, the pilot had been captured alive. Washington said that a spy plane "probably" had been captured but it did not authorize the flight. On May 11, Eisenhower said it was a spy flight, and that they would continue.

Khrushchev demanded that the flights be discontinued. Then he canceled Eisenhower's forthcoming visit to the Soviet Union and called off a Paris peace summit. In August, Powers stood trial in Moscow for spying. During the hearing he claimed that he was nothing more than a pawn in the whole operation. He was sentenced to ten years in prison. But on February 10, 1962, he was traded for a German spy who was captured by the United States. After being debriefed by the CIA, Powers was praised when he returned home. But the U-2 incident led to the breakup of an important summit meeting and heated up the Cold War once again.

ups and downs

The U-2 Incident had been a huge embarrassment to Khrushchev. Veiled criticism appeared in the Soviet press for letting Americans have free reign in Soviet airspace. In September 1960, Khrushchev gave a fiery speech to the United Nations complaining about American spying. During a speech by the U.N. Secretary General, Khrushchev caused a scandal by pounding on his desk with a shoe.

On April 12, 1962, Khrushchev scored big when the spaceship *Vostok* carried Yuri Gagarin on a 108-minute journey around the globe. The handsome jet pilot was the first person to orbit Earth. After he ejected at 20,000 feet and descended by parachute, he was welcomed back to the Soviet Union as a national hero.

But trouble was brewing in the Soviet Union. Khrushchev started a purge to get rid of political enemies within the Kremlin. Soviet farmers were still unable to feed the hungry masses.

Yuri Gagarin, the first person to orbit the earth in a Russian spacecraft in 1962.

The economy was a mess, with shops bearing long lines and empty shelves. Food prices rose thirty percent overnight. Workers decided to strike. As in the days of Stalin, people were shot in the street for protesting. Many were rounded up and sent to labor camps. People could not believe such a thing could happen again, ten years after Stalin's death.

The Cuban Missile Crisis was the last straw. When Khrushchev lost the duel between the two superpowers, his political days were numbered. The only town in the Soviet Union bearing his name quickly changed it. For several years, Khrushchev maintained power by easing the restrictions on art and literature. Two weeks after the Missile Crisis, Khrushchev allowed a short story to be published. The story, "One Day in the Life of Ivan Denisovich" was written by Alexander Solzhenitsyn. In it, Solzhenitsyn detailed the horrors of life in one of Stalin's prison camps. With its publication, Khrushchev raised the stakes against the "heirs of Stalin" that were trying to bring him down.

On Khrushchev's seventieth birthday, he was awarded a "Hero of the Soviet Union" medal. Khrushchev said he was pleased with his life and had no intention of stepping down.

Six months later, he was vacationing on the Black Sea when a phone call informed him that he was through. Khrushchev flew to Moscow where he was read an indictment of all his failings. The Communist newspaper Pravda listed Khrushchev's shortcomings: "Harebrained scheming, hasty conclusions, rash decisions, and actions based on wishful thinking, boasting and empty words." Khrushchev's closest advisors had overthrown him. Afterwards, when one of his grandsons was asked what Khrushchev did all day he replied, "Grandad cries."

Khrushchev's successors quickly threw a few bones to the Soviet public to get their approval. They allowed them to expand their farms, distributed extra rations of flour, and announced an extra day for the New Year's Holiday. Stalin's name began to appear again and tributes were paid to him. Out of the faceless crowd in the Kremlin emerged Leonid Brezhnev who was put in charge of returning Stalin as a hero to the Soviet people. Brezhnev had risen through the ranks of the Communist Party entirely because of Khrushchev, who promoted him steadily for thirty years. Now Brezhnev put on "the dead man's shoes" to quote a Soviet cliche about how power was passed in the Soviet Union.

After the coup, Khrushchev was continually depressed. Eventually he began to visit Moscow, attending the theater and talking to people in the streets. Most of his old friends shunned him. After seven long years of living in the shadows, Khrushchev died of a heart attack on September 11, 1971. The death of Khrushchev was mentioned in a one-line article in Pravda . He was buried, not in the Kremlin wall like Stalin, but in a small cemetery in a monastery. No Soviet official attended the small funeral.

After the terror of Stalin's reign and the chaos of Khrushchev's reign, the Soviet Union was in for a period of stability. But the openness of Khrushchev's reforms became a memory as the secret police once again rounded up thousands of intellectuals and artists in Moscow.

glossary

airspace — The space above a nation that comes under its control.

ballistic missile — A self-propelled long-range missile that becomes free-falling as it approaches its target.

coup — A sudden overturn of power when one person or group replaces another as leader of a country.

holocaust — The mass murder of large groups of people.

Kremlin — A fortified building in Moscow that contains the government center of the Soviet Union. Also the name used for the entire Soviet government.

stockpile — A reserve supply of something accumulated within a country.

index